MARY Sc

Amazing stories for special girls

Audiobook included - Inspiring stories of children that inspire bravery, dreams, confidence, and the endless potential lying within all of us

Emma Lakehead

Amazing stories for special girls

1st Edition
The author is represented by: Emma Lakehead
Address: Unser Frau 169, 39020 Schnals, Italy
Contact: wegamedia@gmail.com
Year of Publication: 2022
ISBN: 9798354158775
Head of Printing: Amazon KDP Publishing

This book belongs to:

....

Content

Foreword

Think about something you would really love to do. Do you ever believe it is too hard to accomplish? It does not matter what it is. It could be something small or your lifelong dream. There are lots of boys and girls who sometimes believe they cannot do something, just like you.

You know what, though? We can reach our goals and make our dreams come true. The only thing in our way is thinking that it is not possible. That is exactly what happens to the main characters of this magical book. Just like you, they end up facing life while being unsure and filled with doubts.

“Am I gonna make it? Am I good enough? What if it’s too difficult?” Those are the questions that Barbara asks herself, for example. She would like to be a journalist but does not have the means to study. Phillip, meanwhile, wishes to be happy but does not yet know how.

Perhaps, like Charlie, you had to challenge everyone and doubt everything to prove your worth. Do you still remember how you felt back then? Sure, you were afraid, but in the end, you found the strength within you. It allowed you to succeed and to show how special you are—mostly to yourself.

The world spins around so fast that sometimes you just want to push it away. Don't you? Everybody is asking something of you. You end up feeling a tight knot in your stomach. Once in a while, something bad could happen. Something you would have a hard time understanding and explaining. When that happens, you may try and follow Chloe's lead. After feeling down, she learns the value of life and finds strength within herself.

You could also go through a deep and meaningful experience like Jack did. Thanks to empathy and friendship, he learned that being different is not a flaw–it is a value.

Each one of these little kids will take you on a trip into their world. They will share their inspiring stories with you. You will get emotional, have fun, laugh, and think. What about? Everything, but mostly about how our lives can be truly wonderful. That is, if we only allow ourselves to love and be loved.

Life will put challenges in front of you. But whatever they may be, all your fears will suddenly fade away, thanks to these twelve stories. You will find an unexpected strength within you.

When you really want something

Barbara's greatest dream was to write. A pen was the very first thing she had picked up and held in her little hands. Of course, back then, she was just two years old. She could hardly imagine how to use it to write down her thoughts and ideas. But her father would look at the way she held his pen. (Her fists were so cute and tiny, her fingers so chubby and little.) Albert used to say that his daughter would grow up to be a journalist or a writer. He and his wife, Naomi, were very humble and simple people. They had not studied beyond high school. As she was growing up, their beloved Barbara would prove to be really good at school. This made her parents happy and satisfied.

All of Barbara's teachers used to praise her. Now she was about to be a high schooler and she was more and more committed to becoming a journalist. Her chief supporter was her English teacher, Mrs. Lara, who thought her favorite student was very talented. She had often suggested to her parents that they enroll Barbara in the town's best high school. It was known as the best school for kids who wanted to be journalists and writers.

The issue was that this private high school was very expensive. Albert and Naomi knew that they certainly didn't have enough money to send their daughter there. Barbara, on the other hand, did not realize what the problem was. She was sure that at the end of junior high, she would be going to that famous high school.

She didn't think about the money because she had never had to worry about paying a bill. She had no idea how little was left in her parents' wallets at the end of the month. She was not a shallow kid. She was actually a very hardworking and sincere girl. But she did not yet know that in this world, dreams can have a price. And a high one.

Just like that, all Barbara's hope seemed to be lost in one sad evening.

Earlier that day, people from the city's high schools came by to leave brochures about careers. Exams were approaching at school. The kids had to choose what they would be as grown-ups. Of course, Barbara had picked up the only brochure she was interested in.

Later that day, she was sitting at the kitchen table with her mom and dad. "But why can't I go there?" she asked sadly.

"Because we can't afford it, honey," her unhappy mother replied. "Your father and I know how important this is to you. And trust me, we are so sorry. But it's just not possible."

Barbara was not a spoiled and shallow girl. She had always told the truth and looked at things straight in the face. Therefore, she realized that what she wanted was not possible. And instead of being angry at her parents, she understood them completely.

The next day at school, Mrs. Lara saw her looking in low spirits. She sat down next to the girl during break time. "What's going on, Barbara?" she asked her.

The girl told Mrs. Lara about the talk she'd had with her parents the night before. Then she officially announced her decision. "Once I'm done with junior high, I will start looking for a job. I don't want to be a weight on my family."

"What about your dream of being a journalist?" Mrs. Lara asked her.

"Exactly," Barbara replied. She slowly stood up as the bell rang, announcing the end of recess. "It's nothing but a dream."

Mrs. Lara kept on thinking for a few minutes. She realized that, maybe, there was one last thing she could do to help her student. She called an old friend who worked as a teacher in that high school. And she figured out that Barbara could still make her dream come true, if she really wanted to.

The following day, Mrs. Lara took the girl aside. She told Barbara that every year, the high school offered a scholarship. It was for the best students who could not afford to go there.

In order to be considered, Barbara would have to submit an essay about a topic of her choice. It would have to knock the socks off the people assigning the scholarship.

And it would have to be done within a week.
"I'll never make it!" Barbara exclaimed.

"Do you know what the only thing is that prevents you from achieving something?" asked the teacher.

"What?"

"Not believing that you can do it."

After school, Barbara sprinted back home. She did her homework as fast as she could. Then she locked herself in her room and began to write down lots of words. She did some research and finally chose pollution as the topic of her essay. It was a very popular subject around town.

She spent a whole week writing without saying anything to anyone. Then she turned in her essay. Guess what happened? Of course, Barbara became the best student at the famous high school. Ever since that day, she believed that you can achieve something if you really want to. But you can only do that by believing it with all your heart.

Moral of the story:

This story teaches children that nothing can prevent you from getting something you want with all your heart. The only hurdle you have to overcome is your own belief about what you can or cannot do.

I AM ENOUGH

What you get does not matter, what you give does

John and Paul were brothers, but they couldn't have been more different from each other.

John was ten years old. He had blond hair and blue eyes. Paul was eight years old. He had curly, red hair all over his head. His dark eyes were sparkly and sly. John was tall and lanky, while Paul was shorter and chubbier.

What really set them apart was not their appearance, but their character. John was always kind to everyone. He would always say something nice. Most importantly, he would never complain about anything.

Paul was quite the opposite. He was not evil, of course! But he was never satisfied with what he had. Whenever his parents would give Paul a gift, he always felt that John received a better one. Even if John tried to offer him his own gift, it would not matter. Paul would keep on sulking.

Oddly enough, John always appeared to succeed at everything. But nothing ever seemed to work out the right way for Paul. And the more he complained, the worse things would go!

One fateful day, though, something happened that the

two children would never forget.

Their parents took them to a carnival. John and Paul had been wishing to go there for a long time. Finally, their beloved fair had rolled into town. The two brothers were so excited they were bouncing off the walls!

They had agreed to pick up the tickets after school with Mom and Dad. But something unexpected forced their parents to run late. By the time they reached the ticket booth, only two tickets were left. Either Mom or Dad had to get one of the two. The children couldn't possibly visit the carnival on their own. So, who would get the chance to enjoy a world of fun and entertainment?

Their mom, Jenna, suggested they should come back the following year. That way, the whole family could enjoy the carnival together. Unfortunately, Paul began to make a fuss. No matter what, he wanted to go on the roller coaster. He wanted the fortune teller to read his hand, too. Their dad, Frank, tried to explain that only one of the two kids could enter. It would not be fair for either to give the ticket up.

Paul, however, did not listen to reason. He threw another tantrum by stomping his feet on the ground. He also complained. He complained about their parents being late, then about having to wait a whole year just to have some fun.

John, ever the kind soul, gave up his ticket. Even though his parents wanted to wait, Paul would not miss the chance. So, Jenna and John went home, and Frank took Paul on the roller coaster. Then they went to the fortune teller. Here, Paul learned a lesson he would not soon forget.

The fortune teller took his small hand in hers. She gave him such a stern look that the child got a bit spooked. Then, gravely said, “I see that you are a very fussy kid, one who never values anything in life.”

Paul could only gasp. He was lost for words.

Her look growing harsher, the woman kept on pushing the child. “I see, as well, that you always complain about what you already have. Don’t you?”

Paul tried to say something, but the fortune teller was quicker. She wrapped up her speech. “I shall now tell you something really important. I will put a little spell on you that will show you something very special. You should know that there is a force in the world, a kind of magic. It works like this: everything you do comes back to you. Therefore, if you only try to take, you will never be happy. In the next few days, you must only give to others. Perhaps you’ll just say a kind word to somebody. But you’ll have to give.”

Paul found that he was able to speak again. He asked, “What if I don’t want to do it?”

“Then,” finished the fortune teller, “everything will go wrong.”

Paul sprang up from his chair and rushed out of the

fortune teller's tent. His father was waiting for him. They went back home together, but the child kept quiet the whole time. His father asked Paul what the fortune teller had told him but Paul simply pouted in silence.

On their way home, Paul told his dad to buy him pizza. But at the first pizza place, they found out that the oven was broken. Next up was ice cream. This time, after all the fuss he made to get it, Paul dropped the cone. His dad refused to buy him another one. At home, Paul found out that his mom had made roasted chicken and fries. He tried to steal John's chicken thigh. However, the plate fell to the ground and broke. It felt like everything was falling apart!

Paul started to hear the words of that strange fortune teller inside his head. "In the next few days, you must only give to others. Or everything will go wrong."

Then, he tried to do something he had never done before. He tried to give something away without expecting anything in return. He offered John his slice of cake. He also thanked his brother for letting him go to the carnival.

Jenna and Frank couldn't believe it. But Paul went even further. In the following days, he began showing kindness and being helpful. Since then, good things started to come back to him even more.

Moral of the story:

The moral of this short story is rooted in the idea of karma. Every deed, either good or bad, will be rewarded with an equal result. That is why it is so important to give rather than simply take. This is how you will get good things in return.

I AM LOYAL

I want to be happy when I grow up

The last day of school had finally arrived. All the children sitting inside the classroom were waiting with joy for the last bell, the bell that stood between them and the much-longed-for summer holidays.

Mrs. Fontaine was very proud of her students. In their

first year together, they had always paid attention during her classes. They were willing to study, learn new things, and they had very high energy. Sure, they were still too young to know what they would grow up to be.

Mrs. Fontaine, though, knew young people so well. (She had been teaching for forty years.) And she was aware that this was the right time to teach them something really important.

It does not matter what you do with your life. What really matters is what makes you happy.

So, Mrs. Fontaine assigned the same task she did at the end of every school year. She was confident that the upcoming summer would have wonderful surprises in store for everyone.

"My dear kids," she began that morning. "As you already know, today is the last day of school. Today, I want to give you a special task . . ."

She did not get a chance to finish as everyone began to complain.

"Please calm down, kids. I know you have already done a lot of homework during the year. And you have all been very good. But the task I want to give you right now is quite special. I am sure you will love it. This summer, you will have to do whatever you like best!"

The students were completely stunned. They started looking at each other.

The teacher was expecting that kind of reaction. It was the very same that all of her students had. Then she stood up and began to walk around the classroom. She gently patted the kids' heads while she explained what that task actually meant. "I know you are still very young," she said. "But if I asked you who you want to be when you grow up, what would you answer?"

Everyone started shouting. Someone said they wanted to be an astronaut. Others said they wanted to be a pilot, or a dancer.

"All right, calm down, kids! Okay, people always say these things. Everyone wants to be a pilot or a dancer. But are you sure that's what you really want?"

The children could not find an answer. That question had taken them by surprise.

Phillip sat silently in the back of the classroom. Mrs. Fontaine asked him, "What about you, Phillip? What would you like to be when you grow up? Is there anything you would like to do?"

Phillip's bright blue eyes looked back at the teacher. He replied, "I want to be happy when I grow up."

For a whole minute, the teacher said nothing. Then she asked, "And what would you like to do to be happy?"

The other students kept on watching the scene in respectful silence.

"Well, that's the issue. I don't know," Phillip answered. Things were starting to get interesting. And this was the very reason the teacher had assigned the task she had. She said, "Well, Phillip, and everybody else as well. This is exactly what I would like you to do this summer. Figure out what makes you happy. You can spend time with your friends, try out a sport that you enjoy, read, write. You could also spend some time with your parents to observe them as they work. In other words, cook, play, dance. Do whatever you want to figure out what truly makes you happy."

That was Mrs. Fontaine's task for summer vacation. When the bell finally rang, all the students left the classroom, rushing toward a warm and lovely summer.

During the following few months, they all carried out the task and learned something interesting. For example, Abigail always used to say she wanted to be a dancer. She asked her parents to sign her up for a summer dance class. They were very happy. However, Abigail realized that being a dancer meant giving up other things. It also meant a lot of exercise. Since she was a little lazy, she realized it would not be the best choice for her future.

On the other hand, Charlotte spent the summer holidays with her grandparents. They owned a wonderful and plentiful vegetable garden. Charlotte's parents had important jobs downtown, so they were always very busy. But Charlotte came to value the slow and quiet pace of country life. She made up her mind to keep working at her grandparents' huge country house. She would take care of the colorful vegetable garden and the sweet-scented vineyard.

When the students came back to school in September, they were all excited. They couldn't wait to share their fabulous experiences with the teacher. Luke, for instance, had always been a shy kid. He found out that he loved to write. Mrs. Fontaine, though, was really curious to know what Phillip had to say.

"Well, Mrs. Fontaine," he replied with the wisdom of his eleven years. "When I grow up, I want to be a teacher!"

"Okay, how did you come up with this idea? After all, it's a job like any other, isn't it?"

"To be honest, you told us to find out what makes us happy," said Phillip. "And I feel happy when I can make other people happy. When I am a teacher, I will be able to assign this wonderful task to all my students!"

That was the most beautiful "thank you" the teacher had ever heard.

Moral of the story:

The moral of this story is that you can only be happy if you truly understand yourself. What really matters is that what we are doing makes us happy and grateful to be alive.

I AM GOOD

The thanking game

Ms. Ashley walked into the classroom to teach her young students. Her class stood out as one of the politest classes in the school. Her students also had the very best grades in all subjects. However, the teacher had a major concern.

One of her students, Eddy, had never said, "thank you." Eddy was not a bad kid. Quite the opposite, actually. He would always deliver his homework right on time. He scored well on every test. Yet, he would never thank anyone when he received something. If one of his classmates shared a book with him, he would take it for granted.

Ashley could not stop thinking about how to make up for this flaw. It was important to her. Ever since the first day of school, all her students would stand up when the principal walked into the classroom. They would say "hello," "please," and "thank you." However, Eddy looked like a lost cause.

One day, Ms. Ashley was meeting with the children's parents. Eddy's father, Mr. Johnson, showed up at the meeting. Right off the bat, he presented himself in a very rude way. He ordered Ms. Ashley to tell him why he had been asked there. He had a very important job to do and no time to waste.

Ms. Ashley explained that she wanted to talk about his son, Eddy. The man blurted out, "What did he do?"

"Nothing!" the teacher quickly replied.

"Why did you call me, then?" Mr. Johnson growled.

"I just wanted to let you know that Eddy never says thank you. He seems to think he deserves everything," Ms. Ashley answered.

Mr. Johnson remained silent for a few seconds. Then his eyes widened, and he went on. "But he gets good grades, doesn't he?"

"Yes, but . . ." Ms. Ashley began to answer.

"Look," Eddy's father interrupted her. "I just don't understand what the issue is. Eddy is doing well at school. He never thanks others. So what? Whom should he say thank you to? Everything we own, we built ourselves. We don't have to say thank you to anybody!"

Afterward, he stormed out, leaving the teacher all alone. It was then that Ms. Ashley figured it out. Eddy had picked up his rudeness from his father.

Mr. Johnson was a very wealthy man. He believed that he should not be grateful to anyone just because he had earned a lot of money. Poor Eddy. If things did not change soon, he would become just like his father.

Now, the teacher knew exactly what she ought to do. She thought about a neat little trick that would do wonders for both father and son.

The following day, Ms. Ashley walked into the classroom. She had a bright smile on her face.

"Hello, children," she began. "Today we are going to play a fun game called 'the thanking game'! Here is what you need to do. All day, you have to say thank you whenever someone is nice to you. It does not matter whether they do you a huge favor or just tell you good morning. You have to say thank you every single time. But that is not all. You will play this game in pairs. You, Eddy, will play with Matthew."

Ms. Ashley had thought of everything. If she had told

only Eddy to say thank you all day long, it would have been useless. But she had paired him with Matthew, the kindest child in the entire school. The plan might just work.

"This game is meant to show you something very important," she explained. "Whenever you thank someone, that person will be happy. They will, in turn, thank someone else. This way, the kindness will be shared. A simple 'thank you' will create a lot of happiness. Do you understand, children?"

Eddy said something under his breath, but everyone else was happy to play. Especially Matthew. He started to thank everyone for everything, right next to Eddy.

Eddy was keeping quiet. But every time someone thanked him, he had to admit that he felt a little happier. Even if it was for just a small, meaningless act.

So, he gave it a try on the way home. He said a big thank you to the man who used to take the milk to his house.

The milkman had grown used to the Johnsons treating him coldly. But that afternoon, he felt his heart lift an inch or two.

Later that evening, something unexpected left Eddy speechless. His father came home after work with a tray of tasty sweets. He never did this. "What's with the surprise?" his wife asked him.

"Something very lovely happened today," Mr. Johnson replied. "I stopped by the milkman's to settle the bill. And the boy thanked me at least a dozen times. I asked him why he was in such a good mood. He replied that a kid was kind to him today. So, he wanted to return that kindness."

Eddy was moved by this story. He understood right away that he was the kid mentioned by the milkman. It happened just like the teacher had said. His own kindness created the milkman's kindness toward his dad. And then his dad had felt so good that he had come back home with sweets.

The next day, Eddy was the first to stand up when Ms. Ashley entered the classroom. He went up to her and gave her a kiss on the cheek. Then he whispered, "Thank you."

Moral of the story:

The moral of this story is that being kind to others makes others happier as well. It sparks a positive mood that spreads the happiness around for everyone to enjoy.

I AM HONEST

History, as told by grandparents

Little nine-year-old Rachel was riding the school bus home from school. She was thrilled by the task that the teacher had given the class.

She walked into the large apartment where she lived. Her mother was waiting for her in the kitchen. Her father was still at work but her grandparents were sitting comfortably in the living room, reading a book. They lived in the apartment with the rest of the family.

"Mom, Mom!" cried the little girl.

"What is it, darling?" her mother, Rose, answered. She was getting lunch ready.

Rachel flew into the kitchen, quick as lightning. She threw herself into her mother's arms. Rose returned her loving hug. Then she asked, "Aren't you going to say hello to your grandparents?"

Rachel freed herself from her mother's arms and rushed into the living room. Grandpa Tony and Grandma Mary were waiting for her with joy. "Hello there, Rachel," her grandmother greeted her. "How was school today?"

"All good, yeah," the kid quickly replied.
"And did you learn anything interesting?" asked her grandfather.

“Oh, lots of new things. But I’m sure you’re not interested in them. We had computer class,” said the little girl, ending their chat.

Rachel loved her grandparents so much. But she didn’t talk with them a lot. She believed they were “ancient,” as her best friend Bea always said. In the eyes of the children, everyone over thirty years old was *old*. (This was a word Mom had told her many times not to use.) But her grandparents, well, they were real dinosaurs. Rachel would chat with them at the dinner table. But never for long, and definitely not about the wonders of the Internet. That was exactly the task that the teacher had assigned to the students that day.

It excited Rachel so much. She was supposed to write a short essay on the 1970s by the following day. There was no point in talking to her grandparents. They didn’t use the Internet. And as far she knew, they didn’t even know what it was.

Lunch went by quietly. Swinging her little legs under the table, Rachel ate quickly. She couldn’t wait to start working on her essay. She had only just been allowed to use the Internet, always under the watchful eye of her mom. But ever since she first tried it, she just could not live without it. Her mom would try to talk her into using books sometimes, but to Rachel, anything that was not connected was indeed ancient.

That's why what happened later that day taught her a lesson she would never forget.

Once she was done eating her fruit, the girl got up from the table. She rushed to her mother's study where the computer was. She sat on a chair and shouted, "Mom! Come here! We gotta do research!"

Mom looked into the room with a towel in her hands. "No Internet for today, honey. The technicians are changing the cables. There will be no connection available until tomorrow."
"What?!" cried the worried kid. "What am I supposed to do now? I have to turn in my research tomorrow morning!"

Rose smiled at her and said, "See? Now you have to use books, don't you?"

Rachel snorted and pouted. "I don't know how to do that, and it takes too long anyway." She was feeling more and more annoyed, so she started to whine. "I'll go to Bea's to do the research!"

Rose calmly tried to explain to her that no one could take her to Bea's. Meanwhile, the grandparents, who had heard everything, had already found the answer.

Mary and Tony walked into the study holding something in their hands. It wasn't a book, but a photo album. (One of the "ancient" ones, as Rachel would call it.) It had lots of printed photographs.

"We can help you," Tony told his granddaughter. He sat down on the sofa, and Mary joined him. Hesitantly, Rachel followed them. Rose went back to her chores.

Rachel could not have imagined what that fateful

afternoon had in store for her.

Photos in hand, her grandparents began to tell her everything about the 70s. They had not read about it on the Internet. They had actually lived through those years. They had experienced all the changes and fears.

They described the fashion and trends of the time to little Rachel. She saw photos of the famous bell-bottoms she had only ever seen on the Internet. Grandpa and Grandma illustrated what life was like back then. They brought back their own memories of the moon landing and what they felt when it happened. They showed her what postcards looked like at that time. They explained what it was like before the Internet and smartphones. Back then, you had to walk to the phone booth whenever you wanted to call someone.

But the most important lesson they taught her was this: when things are always available, they often end up losing their real value.

In wonder, Rachel was completely focused on her grandparents' words. She started looking at them through different eyes. The essay they wrote together ended up earning her an A! And since then, whenever Rachel had a question, she would first ask her grandparents before looking on the Internet.

Moral of the story:

This story has two morals. First, it lets us understand how important it is to look for your own information. It's good to be free from technology. Second, it teaches us the value of the wisdom that our grandparents can share with us.

I AM STRONG

Time is (not always) money

LaMarcus Williamson was lying in a large and comfortable armchair in his father's study. While his father talked on the phone, LaMarcus colored his sketchbook. Still, he could not help but listen.

"Time is money!" his father yelled into the phone. He

was talking to the secretary. It seemed she was taking too long to write a report.

LaMarcus put the pencil down on the wooden table. He looked at his dad, who was making gestures and yelling loudly. LaMarcus often felt rather upset when his father acted that way, but after time, he grew pretty much used to it. As a lawyer, his father was always working on an important case. He never had time to spare for his son. Not even when—as on that day—they were together.

It did not even matter that it was LaMarcus's birthday. It didn't matter that his father had said he would have whatever he wished for. "Ask me anything you want," his dad had said. "Today, I will grant your every wish."

LaMarcus was playing all alone. His father hardly spoke to him. LaMarcus had heard his dad repeat the phrase "time is money" a million times. He did not know exactly what that meant. At seven years old, money was something he did not have to worry about yet. Still, he had figured out that in life, nothing was ever free. (This was another phrase his father used often.)

LaMarcus's father, George, was not a greedy or stingy man. Quite the contrary, he always spent a lot of money, both on himself and on his family. But he seemed to measure people by the amount of money they had. He could afford everything thanks to his money. And if someone didn't have enough money, he thought they hadn't been good enough to earn it. That's why this kind of person was worth very little in his eyes.

This line of thought would have scarred LaMarcus deeply. But life—as usual—found a way to teach everyone a good lesson.

Lawyer Williamson was supposed to meet his last client for the day. When the client entered the room, the secretary told Williamson his name. The lawyer kept looking at the client for a short while. Then he got up and invited the client to sit down. He paid no attention to his own son. He didn't ask the client if the child's presence bothered him.

As the man sat down, he winked at LaMarcus. The boy looked dumbstruck, pencil in the air.
The client was a funny-looking older man. He wore a red and blue plaid shirt and a straw hat on his head. As he began to speak, LaMarcus's dad eyebrows rose in surprise. He burst out laughing.

"So," George began. "You're telling me that you want to ask one of the best lawyers in town for advice. But you don't have the money to pay me?"

"Actually, that's not what I said," the old-timer corrected him. "I just said I can't pay you in cash. But I have something much more valuable to give you."

LaMarcus's eyes moved back and forth from his dad to the nice old man.

"And what would this thing be? Diamonds? Shares? Oil?" asked the lawyer.

"Nope," answered the old man. "Time."

Lawyer Williamson sat silent for a few seconds. Then he laughed again and asked the gentleman to leave.

It was then that LaMarcus shouted, “This is my gift!” He was unable to explain why he had said it.

“What now?” his father asked him. The old man was smiling at LaMarcus.

LaMarcus got up from his chair, his fists tightly clenched. “You told me I can have whatever I want today because it’s my birthday. I want you to help this kind man who is gonna give you back time!” He said.

Lawyer Williamson was shocked. But there was no way to change his son’s mind. He agreed to help the man with his lawsuit.

What happened next changed the life of George and his son forever.

The old man was actually the CEO of a “time bank.” This

was a special kind of bank where time is traded instead of money. People help others by doing something for them. For example, Bill the plumber would fix everyone else's pipes. In return, he would receive a cake from Julie and a handmade sweater from Faith. Sophie the dentist would take care of other people's teeth. In return, she got fruit and vegetables from Horace's garden. Everybody offered their own time and talents.

And that is how the old man, Joshua, would pay the lawyer. He would help George's son with his own skills. Joshua had noticed how much LaMarcus loved to draw. Since he was an art teacher, Joshua promised to give him free lessons. In return, he would get legal help from George.

At first, George was against the idea. In time, he changed his mind under continued pressure of his son.

One evening during dinner, the lawyer asked his son why he behaved the way he did. LaMarcus's reply left him shell-shocked once again.

"You see, Dad," LaMarcus wisely said, "you always say that time is money. But if one day you lost all your money, I would still love you anyway! Well, Joshua has little money. And if what you'd said were true, he wouldn't be loved by anyone. And that's not fair. Time is not money," LaMarcus concluded. "It's love."

Moral of the story:

This story aims to help children understand that money is not everything. There are things such as love, bravery, and unity that cannot be bought.

I AM SPECIAL

What goes around comes around!

Jack was a bully. There was no other name for him. Even though he was just twelve years old, he enjoyed being mean to his classmates. He made fun of them all the time. For instance, someone would show up at school with a brand-new backpack.

Jack would make the poor kid give it to him. Or another classmate had received a new smartphone as a gift. Jack would order the kid to let him use it. He wasn't violent, at least not as much as you would think. He was very tall and muscular for his age. So, he hardly ever needed to start a fight. It was enough for him to overpower others physically to frighten them. Then he could talk them into giving him a snack, money, or anything else.

That wasn't all, though. The worst part was that Jack mainly bullied children who were less lucky than he. For example, one of his schoolmates used to stutter. Jack would never miss the opportunity to make fun of him. He would go up to him and ask him a question. When the kid tried to answer, Jack would start to copy him. Then the child would turn red and run away crying.

It looked like nothing could make Jack stop. His teachers had already tried to punish him and give him bad grades. But Jack didn't even bat an eyelid. The principal called his parents over for a meeting at the school. That didn't take care of the issue either. Jack didn't lack education or reasoning skills. What he lacked was a priceless gift that, unfortunately, not everyone has. That gift was empathy.

As fate would have it, one day a little girl joined Jack's class. She had lost her sight in an accident. Mrs. Wheatley, Jack's teacher, was worried when she learned that the girl would be joining the class. She would be one of Jack's classmates. Mrs. Wheatley was certain something bad would happen.

Sure enough, Jack started to bully Anne right away. (That was the girl's name.) He would always be very mean to her, playing awful tricks for no reason at all. One day he threw a pencil at her. Of course, Anne could not catch it because she could not see. Mrs. Wheatley was about to lose her temper. But Anne proved to be very mature for her age. In front of the whole class, she said, "Mrs. Wheatley, don't be angry. Unfortunately, Jack has no idea what it means to not be able to see. If he knew, he would no longer make fun of me."

Once she was back home, the teacher thought about what Anne had said that morning. She suddenly figured out how she could turn around Jack's conduct.

The following day Mrs. Wheatley walked into the classroom. She sat down as usual and addressed her students. "So, kids," she began. "As you know, we are getting closer to the end of the school year. Just like any other year, it is time for you to take the final exam. You also know that every year, you will have to do a task outside the classroom. For example, last year Jennifer wrote a beautiful paper after studying at the public library in her neighborhood. She deserved an A."

Jack blew a raspberry from his chair in the back of the classroom.

The teacher went on. "Bethany also got an excellent grade. She wrote an essay about the home for the elderly she had attended for two weeks."

Then Jack burst out laughing.

Mrs. Wheatley was about to lose her temper again. But she was sure her idea would work this time, so she kept talking. "I will now give you the details about the place you will visit for the next two weeks."

Then she handed out a piece of paper to each student. When Jack received his assignment, he sprang from his chair. "Hey!" he yelled. "What kind of dumb joke is this?"

"It's not a joke, Jack. And if you won't complete your task, you will fail the year," Mrs. Wheatley replied.

Jack knew that he had no choice. His parents could overlook a lot of the things he did, but not a failure at school. He also knew that if he failed, he wouldn't get the brand-new smartphone he wanted. Jack had no choice. He would spend the next two weeks in a center for the blind.

What happened during those days, however, deeply changed the boy's life and heart. Often, in order to understand something, we should not use strength or force. Rather, we should use love and understanding.

Some of the people at the center were children just like Anne. Each child was taught how to dress, wash themselves, read Braille, and be as independent as possible.

When Jack arrived on the first day, Anne went up to the director. She asked him to let Jack spend the day beside her. She was planning something that Jack would never forget.

Anne asked her classmate to put himself in her shoes. Jack replied, "What are you talking about?" Anne told him that every day he came to the center, he'd have to do everything blindfolded. Jack laughed. He said that it would be a piece of cake for him.

However, he bumped into every corner. He was not able to pick up anything with his own two hands. And then something inside him changed for the better. He finally realized that making fun of others is wrong.

From that day on, Anne became his best friend.

Moral of the story:

The most meaningful changes can only happen when we put ourselves in other people's shoes.

I AM COURAGEOUS

An unforgettable party

Everything was ready for the huge party that Mr. Alfredsson had planned.

Mr. Alfredsson was one of the many people living in a quiet and charming town. Tony and Jessie also lived there. Everyone liked the twin brothers because they were always kind and smiling. Everyone except for Mr. Alfredsson.

The reason, as it happens, was silly. Mr. Alfredsson could not stand the boys because of an accident. It had taken place a few weeks earlier. Jessie and Tony had been playing catch in the yard. They mistakenly threw the ball over the hedge, breaking the glass in Mr. Alfredsson's porch window. The two children had quickly said they were sorry. Their father had offered to pay to fix the glass but Mr. Alfredsson was still angry.

Mr. Alfredsson was running for mayor. So, he decided to throw a big party in the yard but he did not invite the twins.

"Such a rude man!" tthe boys' mother, Sarah, complained. "An adult should not act like this. Not inviting them was really nasty." Tony and Jessie's mom was right. (Even more so because the children attended the same class as Mr. Alfredsson's son, Edward.)

"Don't even think about it," her husband comforted her. "Don't stoop down to his level."

However, Sarah felt sad for her children. They were playing alone in the yard. Meanwhile, the first guests showed up in front of the mansion next door. They were smartly dressed people who wanted to cozy up to the future mayor. They began to get out of expensive-looking cars. Throughout the evening, the family kept hearing loud laughter and shouting. Music and singing also came from the other side of the hedge.

To be honest, Jessie and Tony were not that upset about the whole thing. They were playing on their own, that was true. They lacked nothing. They loved each other and were loved by their parents. They had everything they could want. Their house was rather small compared to Mr. Alfredsson's but it was full of love and the tasty scent of the cakes their mom made.

Jessie and Tony mulled over these things in their minds. (They were twins, so they often thought the same way.)

As they did, they suddenly heard a loud explosion. Then lots of screams came from the mansion next door. A cloud of smoke rose from beyond the hedge. Shortly after, a large crowd of people rushed out of Mr. Alfredsson's yard. It didn't take long for the firefighters to get there. They unleashed their powerful hoses over the whole house.

Here's what had happened. An electric wire fixed to the garden lights had caught fire. It turned the entire yard to ashes, along with the wooden fence and gate. It also ruined the porch and its wall.

Mr. Alfredsson was standing in the street, hands in his hair. He complained about his bad luck. Then, he started asking whether anyone was hurt. When he was sure that everyone was unharmed, he sat down on the sidewalk.

Looking at his house going up in smoke, he realized something. No one was there anymore. All those people had worked so hard to be at his party. They had praised him and tried to cozy up to him, but they left as soon as he got into trouble. All of a sudden, he felt very alone. His wife had left him a while ago, telling him that he was a selfish man. She had taken Edward away. His own son didn't even want to attend that party.

Mr. Alfredsson was realizing just how rude he had been to everyone. Then something completely unexpected happened. Four people popped out from the house next door. It was Tony and Jessie, the blameless children he disliked, and their parents. Sarah carried a baking tray full of hot pizza. Her husband, Paul, was wearing work overalls. Tony and Jessie each held a colorful balloon.

At first, Mr. Alfredsson did not understand what was happening. But as soon as the children began to speak, he was deeply touched by their words. A waterfall of tears began to run down his cheeks.

"These balloons are for you," Jessie said as he held them out. "So, you can keep on celebrating."

"This is hot pizza that I had made for dinner tonight,"

said Sarah. "We can eat it together."

"And I called my coworkers from the construction company," said Paul. "They are coming to fix your yard. In the meantime, you can come sleep at our place tonight."

Mr. Alfredsson could not believe his ears. He felt so happy and grateful. And ever since that fateful day, he treated Tony and Jessie as his favorites. He always invited them as guests of honor to all his parties.

Moral of the story:

The moral of this story is that grown-ups may look and sound mean sometimes. But truth be told, they have just forgotten how important friendship, love, and kindness are.

HAPPINESS IS A CHOICE

The true "nature" of life

Chloe was a really sweet girl. She had long red hair and bright green eyes. She always looked out at the world full of spirit and joy. She was ten and had always been a healthy child. Yes, she was a greedy eater. She would often eat ice cream, chocolate, and candies. She would regularly drink sugar-filled drinks. But she also played sports, as she was on her school volleyball team so she wasn't overweight.

That is why the day she fell ill was a very sad and unexpected day for her family.

It all happened so fast that her mom and dad almost didn't realize it. All of a sudden, they received a phone call from the school. They were warned about Chloe's health. She had a bad stomachache and was very thirsty. She had also passed out.

The doctors looked Chloe over as soon as her parents took her to the hospital. Afterward, they told her mom Charise and dad Daniel that she had diabetes.

That word came as a complete shock to them. There had never been similar cases in their family. How could a ten-year-old girl have such a scary disease?

The doctors tried to explain two things to them. First of all, Chloc was young and had plenty of time to change

her lifestyle. Secondly, the disease was not at an advanced stage yet. This allowed the family to hope that her good health would return.
Of course, Chloe would have to turn her diet around. No more candies, sweets, or sugary drinks. She would have to get checked regularly and be more careful. The doctors also said that Chloe should go to a class with other children who had the same disease. They claimed that it would help her accept her condition.

In fact, Chloe was awfully upset. First, she cried. Then she got angry about what had happened to her. Finally, she said that she didn't care. She would keep eating whatever she wanted. Her parents tried to talk sense into her but there was no point in trying.

However, there was no way around it. Chloe's life totally changed overnight. Things that she had done without any issues up until that day had become dangerous. She was always checking her blood sugar level. She couldn't eat an extra slice of cake at her classmate's birthday party. She couldn't get too tired. In short, it is quite understandable that she felt sad, scared, and angry.

Chloe started hanging out with other children who had the same condition. Then, she started feeling a little relieved. She no longer felt lonely. She could talk to other children who were going through the same thing. They felt the same emotions she did. All this helped her a lot.

The help she received from one child, Jade, was very important. Jade was a high-spirited eleven-year-old girl. She had a cheerful face and a sharp mind. She had recently grown her own vegetables.

The doctors had told Jade that she had to change her diet a while ago. Ever since then, the smart kid had begun to read every book she could find about diabetes. She learned what she was and was not allowed to eat. For example, she had learned that fruit and vegetables are perfectly fine for diabetic children (as long as they do not eat too many of them.) Of course, she also needed to avoid the ones filled with sugar.

So, Jade started to plant tomatoes in a small vegetable

garden. Her father had prepared it for her at home. She also planted some zucchini and a small apple tree. She cared for the tree with love, waiting for it to bear fruit.

One day, Jade invited Chloe over. The two girls started playing in the garden.

Chloe basically rose from the ashes that day. She spent her time alongside Jade, who explained everything about fruits and vegetables to her. Jade told her which were good for her health. She explained how to grow and cook them. At the end of the day, Chloe asked her mom for a vegetable garden at home. Her mother looked so happy after hearing that!

In the following days, Chloe's family was busy working the soil in their small garden. They tilled the ground and planted seeds that would soon sprout zucchini, tomatoes, lettuce, cucumbers . . . Chloe wished to plant lots of different vegetables. She looked reborn. Nothing else could have made her parents happier.
She slowly regained her energy and brightness, which

were so typical of her. Every day after school, she would work in her small garden. And every morning after breakfast, she would rush to check whether any new plants had grown overnight.

But that was not all. Chloe also learned everything about vegetable gardens and their benefits. She began to write down all the growing patterns of the plants in a notebook. She wrote about how they should be watered, planted, pruned, and cared for. She filled many notebooks in a very short time.

It almost looked like she had forgotten all about her illness, but that wasn't the case. Chloe still felt sad sometimes. This often happened when she realized she could no longer do things she used to like. Yet, at the same time, she also appeared more mature, more peaceful. She explained why to her parents.

"You see, I'm not sick," she said one day. "I'm just different. But I'll take care of myself as I take care of these plants. Then I, too, will become strong, just like them!"

Moral of the story:

The moral of this story is that illness can be a part of life. But that doesn't mean you should just give up. When something scary happens to us, we can turn the situation around and turn it into a priceless gift.

I AM DEDICATED

What really matters is not to win but to help each other

The day of the relay race was fast approaching. All the students were very excited. They had been working hard for months to get ready for the big event. Among them, Charlie was definitely the most thrilled. He was the smallest kid in his class, both height-wise and age-wise. He had changed schools halfway through the year, and he struggled a bit to fit in. However, he was always hard-working, lively, and nice to others. That's why his new classmates had already welcomed him after just a few weeks.

Charlie was very good at gym class. He was so good that Mr. Barlett asked him to become part of the relay team. The city schools would face each other within two months at an official track meet. Charlie had just joined the school, while his classmates had been working hard for some time. But the teacher thought it would be the best way to help the boy fit in.

Charlie was excited. At the same time, he felt how important his task really was. He would be the fourth student during the race, the one who would have to lead the team to victory by crossing the finish line first. He was very good at running. But his teammates still had quite a few doubts.

What if Charlie wasn't that good? What if he got excited at the worst possible time? What if he just blew all the work of the past few months?
Charlie wanted to show them that he could really make it. Even more, he wanted to show Mr. Barlett that the teacher's trust was well placed. So, Charlie began to train very hard. Every day after class, he would stay late at school. He would run on the red clay track. No matter if it rained or if it was sunny, Charlie would train.

Mr. Barlett would watch him from the stands. More and more, he was sure that he had made the right choice. Word soon spread among Charlie's teammates. They began to watch him together with the coach.

One day, the team captain, Ricky, was observing everything from up high. He noticed that Charlie looked pretty tired. So, he decided to go on the field. The captain was afraid that Charlie was feeling down, as he was running all alone. Ricky caught up with him on the track. He started running beside him, cheering him on.

"Come on Charlie!" Ricky shouted at him. "You can do it! Run! You're awesome!"

Charlie got all his energy back thanks to that heartfelt gesture. One by one, the other teammates also came down from the stands. They all started training together.

Mr. Barlett smiled and quietly left the field. He was aware that his coaching job was over, at least the most important part. He now had a real team, and Charlie was part of it.

The day of the meet was getting closer and closer. All the students were in high spirits. Most classes were called off that day, and the meet would take place at Charlie's school. His class had won the grand prize several years earlier. Even third place would have been enough to make them happy.

The qualifying round started. The different teams raced each other, one by one. Charlie's team seemed to have no equals. Thanks to his efforts, it looked like they had a good shot at winning the final prize.

The time of the final race finally came. Charlie's team had to face the strongest team yet. And that's when something very sad and awful happened. Something that may have risked the whole event.

An envious kid kicked Charlie in a sudden fit of anger. This boy had run for a team that was no longer in the race. He hit poor Charlie in the shin, hurting him a lot. Everyone stopped right away. The guilty boy was hauled out of there by his parents. They told him they would deal with him once they were back home.

Harm, however, had been done. Charlie's coach suggested they call off the race for the time being. But Charlie refused. He told Mr. Barlett that he would make it to the end. And so, the final match began.

Near the end of the race, Charlie took the baton from the captain. He then started feeling a sharp pain in his leg. Gradually, he slowed down. He clenched his teeth.

Charlie was bent on making it to the finish line, no matter what. He could not give up right now. His classmates had trusted him so much and welcomed him as a friend. He did not want to disappoint Mr. Barlett, who had always believed in him. Nor did he want to disappoint his parents, who were watching him nervously from the stands.

However, the pain was becoming unbearable. Charlie truly thought he wouldn't make it. Then something happened that silenced the entire arena. It taught everyone there a lesson they would never forget.

The kids who were running the final part of the relay beside him had noticed Charlie. One after the other, they began to slow down. They were matching his pace. Charlie was so moved that he was almost crying. Truly, though, he had been the first person to show sportsmanship that day.

In the end, they all reached the finish line at the same time, hand in hand. The meet had four winners for the first time. Though in fact, good sportsmanship and fair play were the real winners that day.

Moral of the story:

This tale shows kids that winning does not really matter. It's definitely not as important as playing fair, helping each other, and putting ourselves in other people's shoes. This is what winning is really about.

I AM EMPATHIC

To love someone means to take care of them

Michelle truly was a lucky child. She had everything she could ever want. Somebody could have said she even had too much. Her parents were very rich, and they spoiled her. Yet, they were also aware that they were lucky. Sure, they always let their beloved daughter have anything she wanted. But they were always looking for ways to teach her the value of what they did, too.

Bruce and Vanessa were "self-made" people. Starting from nothing, they had created an empire in the technology field. They quickly became quite famous and—more importantly—very rich. When Michelle was born, she had found everything ready for her. She had never experienced the tough times that had scarred her parents before her birth.

Bruce and Vanessa were well aware of the actual value of money and they wanted Michelle to learn that all things had to be earned. What they cared about most was teaching their little girl that love cannot be bought. But Michelle risked becoming a tad too spoiled. Despite being good people, her parents often let her have her way. "I want that!" This was the sentence Michelle used to say most often. As an eight-year-old, she really had everything a kid would ever wish for.

Her mom or dad would say that she was too small to own the latest tablet. They would say that she didn't need another doll. When this happened, Michelle would start crying. She would say, "Then you don't love me!" Without fail, Mom and Dad would give up, and Michelle would get whatever she wanted. They needed someone to teach her that to love does not mean to buy.

That someone knocked on the Bells' door on a sunny Sunday morning. It was Michelle's grandmother, Rose. She wished to see her daughter Vanessa, her son-in-law, and above all, her beloved granddaughter. But Grandma Rose only needed a few minutes with the family to realize that Michelle was different. She had changed for the worse since the last time Rose had been there. The child could not be satisfied. And she had figured out how to convince her parents to always let her have her way.

One evening after dinner, Grandma Rose and Vanessa were alone in the kitchen. While Vanessa was washing the dishes, Rose quietly sipped a tasty-looking tea. "You're taking it a bit too far with Michelle, wouldn't you say?" asked Rose.

"What can I say, Mom? I just can't find it in my heart to tell her no. She just looks at me with those big eyes full of tears. And she tells me that if I don't give her what she wants, I don't love her. I just don't know what to do."

Rose remained silent for a few seconds. Then a little spark lit up within her wide, hazel eyes. "Do you remember Billy?" she asked.

"What does the kitten I had as a child have to do with this?" Vanessa held a plate in her hands, looking confused.

Rose kept going. "I remember that you, too, wanted many things as a kid. Of course, your father and I weren't as rich as you and Bruce are. But all children are alike, after all. They must understand that love is always shared no matter what. You can't just buy it. Do you remember how you took care of Billy? Do you remember how worried you were when she got sick?"

Vanessa looked at her mother, smiling. “Are you suggesting that Michelle needs someone to take care of? So, she can understand what it means to truly love someone?”

“My thoughts exactly,” replied Rose. She finished her tea.

The following day was Michelle’s birthday. Vanessa told her daughter that she had a surprise for her. Michelle was full of excitement. She, her mom, and her granny went out together to get her gift. Vanessa assured Michelle that she would absolutely love it. As they arrived at the shelter, Michelle was overjoyed. She had wanted a pet for a long time. And now she could take home the kitten she liked the most! That was the best gift she could ever receive.

She chose a black kitten with bright blue eyes and called him Billy. For the next few days, Michelle and Billy seemed to be joined at the hip. At least, until something happened. Something that Vanessa and Rose had been expecting. Michelle got tired of her new friend, and she began to forget about him.

One evening, Michelle ran downstairs toward the dinner table. She found her mom, dad, and grandma eating. Her plate, however, was not there. Michelle was quite bewildered. "Why isn't my plate here?" she asked. She placed her little hands on her hips.

Her grandma quickly replied, "Did you get Billy his food?"

"Nope. What's the matter?" asked Michelle.

"You'd better check up on him!" her granny suggested.

Vanessa and Bruce were trying hard not to step in. This was Rose's idea, of course. They knew that she was doing it for their daughter's sake. But it was still hard for them not to help Michelle out.

That night, Billy was sick because he hadn't eaten

anything. Michelle spent the whole time next to him. She helped him to eat his food and nursed him until he recovered. When she woke up, she finally realized that to love does not mean to take, but to give. And she was never the same old Michelle ever again.

Moral of the story:

This story shows us that we need kindness, patience, and a lot of love to take care of someone. It also shows children the amount of work their parents do without asking for anything in return.

I AM RIGHT

The eyes of love

Ethan was trying to listen to the teacher, but he just couldn't pay attention. Ms. Johnson was talking about the life of dolphins. But Ethan was looking at the people passing by right outside the window. He was deep in thought as he played his favorite game. This was guessing what those people's lives were like, where they were going, and why.

For example, he could see a lady wearing a funny little hat. She was quietly walking her dog. Ethan imagined that she was going to meet a friend of hers. The two women would chat for some time while sipping cups of tasty tea. Then, a green-haired boy passed by on a skateboard. Ethan imagined his parents scolding him because of that odd hairstyle.

He used to play this game quite often. Unfortunately, he could never find somebody to play with him. His sister Jessica was too old for these "children's games." (At least that's what she said.) Mom was always busy looking after the house. And Dad was always busy working in the office. That's why Ethan would often zone out and start daydreaming.

"Ethan!" He heard a voice yelling his name. It was Ms. Johnson calling him back to the real world. Her voice surprised Ethan. He began to blush as he looked around and saw all his classmates staring at him. "I'm so sorry, Ms. Johnson. I got distracted."

“I noticed,” the teacher replied. “I was explaining the homework you have to do by next week. The theme is the value of kindness. You have to share something you have done out of kindness, without expecting anything in return.”

As he walked down the road back home, Ethan mulled over his teacher’s words. He wondered just how he would carry out the task. How could you do something out of pure kindness when everyone always asked for something in return? He shrugged and told himself that he would come up with an idea in time.

As soon as he was back home, Ethan tried to put his plan in motion. He went to his sister’s room and asked her if he could help her with her homework. But she was busy talking on the phone with her friend, Sheila. She replied by throwing a pillow at him. Then, Ethan tried to ask his mom if he could help her with dinner. She told him to get out of the kitchen and go play. He would only waste her time.

The little boy walked back to his room, upset. But after a few minutes, his mom showed up at the door. She said, "Ethan, I just remembered something you could help me with. Would you kindly go to Mrs. Dawson and bring her the cake I promised her?"

"Good grief!" blurted Ethan, bothered by the sudden request.

Sometimes, Ethan's mom would make a cake for Mrs. Dawson. She was an old lady who lived in the house next door and who could no longer see. Ethan agreed and picked up the tasty-looking cake from the table. Then he went to knock on Mrs. Dawson's door.

After a few seconds, the door opened. The old lady let Ethan in. "Oh dear! What a nice smell!" she said. She sat down in an armchair near the window and covered her legs with a colorful blanket. "So, Ethan," she then added. "What's the latest? Nobody ever comes here."

In the meantime, the curious boy had already started

looking out the window. He was lost in a world of his own.

"Ethan! Are you still there?" asked Mrs. Dawson.

"What?" he replied. "Yeah, sure. I was just looking at the people outside."

"And what do you see?" the curious lady asked. "Unfortunately, I can't see anymore."

Ethan felt very sad for her. So, he decided to try to play his favorite game with her. He looked out the window as a man dressed as a sailor passed by on the street. "A pirate who has just found a treasure chest is walking by right now!" he said aloud.

Mrs. Dawson kept silent for a moment. Then she burst out laughing. "Don't tell me! You also look at people walking by and imagine a life full of adventures for each of them? You know, I used to do it too as a child. But now that I can no longer see, I can't play that game I used to love so much." Her voice was filled with great sadness.

Ethan looked out the window again. "Oh! Now a princess is passing by," he claimed. He had noticed a beautiful girl wearing a fine, colorful dress. "And she is going to a ball."

Ethan and Mrs. Dawson played together the whole afternoon. The young kid enjoyed it very much. He decided to go back often and play with the sweet old lady.

The surprises were not over, though. Mrs. Dawson turned out to be Ms. Johnson's mother. After finding out about what happened, Ethan's teacher gave him an A+ for his kindness. Ethan learned an important lesson: being kind always pays off!

Moral of the story:

This tale helps children to understand that even people

who look very different from us can still give us so much. It also teaches that a natural act of kindness is always appreciated and rewarded.

YOU ARE WONDERFUL!

Epilogue

I truly hope you have enjoyed these fun little stories. I also hope that you can take something out of them and keep it forever within your heart. Perhaps you have even recognized yourself in one of the characters? It is important to realize that we can all be brave. It is also normal to have doubts sometimes. Being wrong and making mistakes are not always negative things. In fact, they can show our inner strength and firmness, if only we can show our feelings to others.

Color the loving pictures

If you liked the pictures, here is a piece of good news. You can download them all by scanning this QR code. Then you can print them. Three extra stories are also available!

Otherwise, you can enter this URL into your browser to download the pictures: https://bit.ly/coloring-pictures

Have fun coloring!

Audiobook

Scan this code with your phone or tablet and enjoy the stories as audio versions. Or click on the following link: https://bit.ly/3rmuXSd

In rare cases, the audiobook may not play. Please try it on another device.

If you still have problems, please send us a message to contact.wegamedia@gmail.com.

Have fun listening!

By the way, I would be extremely grateful if you could spare a minute of your time and write a review on Amazon.

Reviews are essential for freelance authors, since we can only improve our writing by reading your feedback.

Please, take a minute and write down an honest review of this book!

- *Emma Lakehead* -

Made in the USA
Monee, IL
25 November 2022

18458850R00067